The Praying Sales Rep

The
Praying
Sales Rep

18 Power Principles

Keith Manuel

Hidden Pearl Publishing
Pineville, LA

ISBN 978-0-9978465-1-5

For my family whom I love. Wendy, Keith, Jr., Jeremy, and Hannah.

Also, to all who struggled with me in my brief financial services career. If God did not call me to pursue the pastorate and a Ph.D., I would still be taking care of people in this rewarding field with other great men and women who want to change people's financial future.

The Desperate Church Contents

INTRODUCTION

The Praying Sales Rep

One hundred percent of people in sales pray. Maybe not all pray in a traditional sense, but they all plead for a sale to some god. I've talked to people in used car sales who prayed to the parking lot, going so far as to throw an offering of spare change into the lot. One salesperson told me, "If you feed the lot, the lot will feed you!" Interesting concept. At least it will make some kid's day!

I can already hear a comedian twisting the title of the book, "A praying sales rep, don't you mean a preying salesman?" As the comedian, Rodney Dangerfield, was known to say, "I don't get any respect." A salesperson does not have to prey on his/her clients, but prayer is a large part of the sales event.

Everyone wants the answer to one question. "What's in it for me? What's the value of this book?" One value is you'll become a better sales professional. This book is loaded with top sales tips. A second value is found if you have a team of sales professionals. This is a great tool for a Monday morning pep talk or a "thought for the day" conference call. Finally, you're going to grow closer to God. You can't know a client without talking to him or her. Likewise, you can't know God with a vibrant, growing, conversational relationship with him. You will learn to talk to God as you spend time with this work.

Is this a book to make you rich? Yes! Most people in sales never do the 18 Power Principles found in this book. Those who practice these principles are generally the ones who make a lot of money in sales.

Even if you are doing these principles, I can guarantee this book will make you richer than you already are. However, it may not be how you thought it would. I hope God will bless you financially and use you in powerful ways. More than that, I want God to teach you to develop a rich prayer life. Jesus told us gaining treasures in heaven is more important than gaining treasures on earth. Why? Because wealth in heaven lasts forever; wealth on the earth can be stolen or lost. Everything we gain on earth will be in the hands of someone else when we die. But you can talk to God forever.

You may wonder about my background. I worked for three years with a financial services company. I started because I needed extra income when my first son was born. I only wanted to make a little extra money to supplement my work as a pastor of a small church. My income doubled each year in sales. During year three, I felt the Lord leading me to pursue a Ph.D. at a seminary, so I walked away from financial services after much prayer. It was with much agony

INTRODUCTION

that I left this industry because I loved sales and the people with whom I was honored to work. I honestly thought the Lord was going to allow me to shift to sales as my primary career and help churches secondarily. However, it was with joy, I followed the Lord. I have been in love with researching. Preaching. Theology. Sales. God has allowed these passions of sales and service to combine in this book. It was in my study of sales principles that I saw a resemblance to prayer. The application of these principles as a sales rep will make you money. The pursuit of God in prayer will make you rich. The combination of the two is extremely powerful.

Read on and become a praying sales professional.

BELIEVE IN YOUR PRODUCT

Believe in God

Y ou must believe! If you don't believe in your product, you will not become a good salesperson. The old saying is true, "People can smell a phony a mile away." If you do not, or would not own your product, why would anyone else? Don't try to sell me something that is not good enough for you!

"Every sale has five basic obstacles," said Zig Ziglar, "no need, no money, no hurry, no desire, no trust." One way to overcome some common obstacles is to believe in what you are doing. You must trust in your product before you can convince anyone else to trust it.

Once, I switched cellular companies because I could not get the service that I wanted from my old company. I asked two questions to every sales associate that helped me. The first question was, "How long have you been with the company?" The second question was, "Who was your cellular provider before you worked here and why did you switch?" I wanted to know that the associate had embraced the company he or she was asking me to embrace.

The manager of the store I finally selected was exceptionally good at his job. My main concern was to find a company with the equipment to make cellular calls from my house. I apparently reside in the black hole of cellular service. No company I tried worked well from my home. I told the manager I am looking for a company that will allow me to make calls from my recliner. He let me know clearly that his company could meet my needs. I purchased the phone, went home, and immediately dropped five calls in a row from the comfort of my chair. I was furious. The next business day I called the manager. He told me to come back to the store and he would exchange my phone with a different model. When I went back, not only was he prepared with a new phone but also he assured me that if this phone did not work he would personally come to my house, after-hours, with several phones to find one that would work. He sold me. Not by the product but by the manager. When he did what he said he would do, I trusted him.

Just as a client must find trust in a sales associate, we too must find God trustworthy. Do you believe God? Jesus said, "If you ask anything, believing, it will be done for you." Trusting that God will hear you is the key to prayer. Jesus was not kidding about trust. He confronted the obstacle of trust throughout his ministry. His product was peace with God. A person buys peace from Jesus with the currency of belief. Peter said, "Believe in the Lord Jesus, and you will be saved."

Belief is a well that is much deeper than it first appears. The problem with the word "believe" comes from our lack of English words that accurately convey the biblical concept. For instance, we say we believe that Barak Obama is the current president of the United States. Yet has President Obama ever called you to have dinner at the White House? Has he ever asked you, personally, about a policy he was considering? When Jesus talks about belief, he is not merely describing intellectual knowledge. He is describing personal interaction with God and God with you. He wants you to have a personal, intimate relationship with Him.

How can you have that kind of personal relationship with God? It begins with trust. The mystery of the gospel or good news is accessible to you. The Bible has recorded and demonstrated this message for you. Your relationship with God begins with your personal belief. When you realize all people, including you, struggle with sin, you are in a position to find the answer for the struggle. Jesus' first words in Mark's gospel were, "Repent and believe in the good news." Repentance is a change of mind and direction. You make a decision to surrender your life to God. The good news is that Jesus died, was buried, and rose again so that he could remove your sin. He became your substitute in death. He is your hope for heaven. The Bible says if you will ask Jesus to be your Lord and you will believe that he is who he says he is, you will be saved (Romans 10:9-10). If you have never made a commitment of your life to God, I encourage you to stop and pray right now. In that prayer, you simply need to express your belief in Jesus and your commitment of your life to him. Remember what Jesus said, "Repent and believe."

As you begin and continue a relationship with Jesus, you need to talk to him. You communicate with God through prayer. Let me share with you three truths about prayer. The first truth is that God wants you to pray. When God created Adam and Eve, he began to talk to them. He has sought to communicate with everyone since this first couple. He created you for a relationship with Him. That is why when you are alone and deep in thought, you wonder what he is like. You want to know that you can know him. The great news is you can!

The second truth is that anyone can learn to pray. That is a given. The Bible assures us that when we speak to God, he will listen. What if I increase the value of prayer a little? How would you like to pray in a way that will assure an answer from God? You can and I will let you in on the secrets throughout the book.

The final truth is you must believe you are talking to God. Prayer is not whispering to the wind. It is not informing a god who does not know what is going on in his world. Prayer is a conversation with a living God who knows you and cares about you. Like any other relationship, the more you talk to him, the more you will recognize his voice and trust his answers.

Do you want to be a great salesperson? Believe in your product! Do you want to be a great man or woman of prayer? Believe in God.

Prayer Principle
Believe In God

Dear Jesus,

I want to know you. I want to live my life in commitment to your holiness and your way of love. Help me to love others. Help me to show others the benefit of you as I develop my career. Lord, I want my career to honor you. Give me confidence, boldness, and peace as I work today. May I do nothing that will dishonor you or the people I represent.

In Jesus' name,
Amen.

POWER PRINCIPLE TWO

PLAN TO BE PRODUCTIVE

Plan Your Prayer Time

One of the greatest and worst aspects of being in sales is freedom. Freedom carries with it responsibility. The difference between a good person in sales and a great person in sales is how you deal with the lack of structure. You will spend a great amount of time on your own, setting your own schedule. If you do not create at least a semblance of structure and stick to it, you will starve to death.

Create a routine that combines education, administration, and evaluation to make the best use of the down times. A sale is not only about the act of the sale. It is like doing two-a-days in football (practicing twice a day). The times of practice are not the game, but without the practice, you will have no game. Dan Brent Burt said, "Every boxer fights differently, and every salesman has his unique style. But the results are the same — you are either a champion or just another fighter, you either get the sale or you don't. The real key to success is to do those things that will prepare you to be a champion."

You need to learn new things about your products and your market. Don't skip training opportunities. No matter how long you have been doing a job you need to find ways to get better and grow in your field. You need to take care of paperwork, thank you notes, and prospecting lists. You need to learn new closes and new prospecting methods. You need to analyze your presentations, your choice of words, and your time management. Don't allow the times you can't make a sales presentation to become down times or worse, dead times.

Discipline determines your ability to succeed. Few people love discipline. If we were self-disciplined, we would not have fad diets, diet pills, or cosmetic liposuction. Self-discipline is necessary for everything from planning for retirement to taking care of rainy day expenses. Through discipline as a salesperson, you develop the habits necessary for success. When you live a disciplined life, you enact a plan to challenge you throughout the day.

While working toward my doctoral degree, I can't tell you how many times I wanted to quit. It was tough to create deadlines for writing about my research and then sticking to the deadlines. In my job as a pastor, there was always someone to see, something to do, somewhere to go. Writing can wait. Historical research is not nearly as exciting as meeting needs. Until my seat met the seat of my chair, I put nothing on paper. Many students drop out of doctoral work because of the lack of structure given by the university. Universities and seminaries are rethinking their approach to doctoral work by giving the students deadlines that they must meet. To complete the work one must prepare a plan and work the plan.

Prayer is the same way. You must plan to pray. You must intend to pray or you will find activities to replace it. Prayer is vitally important to your personal development and your personal walk with God. Without prayer, you are a spiritual hermit. You are trying to survive without the interaction God intended for you.

When should you pray? The Bible says to pray without ceasing. That means all through your day you should be interacting with God. Jesus chose to pray early in the morning and late in the evening. He would pause to pray when he was in a conversation with his disciples. Meal times were a time for Jesus and the disciples to give thanks for the Father's provision. Anytime is a great time to pray. What time of the day are you at your best? Are you a morning person, afternoon worker, or a night owl. That's when you ought to carve out some time to pray. When you are awake and alert, you can have an extended conversation with God.

How many things are competing for your time? Work consumes a good portion of your time. If you have children, you must schedule time to do what is important to them. Your spouse must be given quality and quantity time. Then activities like recreation, household chores, church activities, and social gatherings press us for more time. It is a wonder we have a moment to sleep or eat. Because of these activities competing for our time, we must be diligent in scheduling a time for prayer. Do not talk yourself into sacrificing your prayer time for any other activity. Examine your schedule. Set your prayer time. Put it on your calendar, labeling it with high importance. Then, be consistent.

A parishioner confronted a pastor about the large amount of time he devoted to prayer. The parishioner argued that there was so much that was necessary to do, administration, visitation, planning, social events, and sermon preparation. How could a pastor spend hours in prayer with so many pressing issues? The pastor responded, "With all of these issues and more, how could I spend any less time in prayer?" With all the events that are taking time from your day, how can you not spend a large portion of time in prayer?

Once you schedule your time for prayer, find ways to protect that time. Get creative. One pastor needed time away from the rigors of the ministry. Because he did not want to offend anyone with his need for relaxation, he found a way to do it gracefully when time allowed. When someone called for the pastor, his secretary would say he was out on visitation. The pastor named his boat . . . Visitation.

Imagine having the opportunity every day to have a private meeting with the CEO of a Fortune 500 company who is committed to your success in life. As great of an opportunity as a meeting with any CEO would be, it does not compare with your ability to speak to God at any moment of any day. The Bible says you can approach the throne of God with boldness if you are his child. Plan to have a private meeting with God today. Don't miss it.

Prayer Principle
Plan Your Prayer Time

Dear Jesus,

I need discipline. At work. At home. With my family. With you. Help me to become a person of deep prayer. Help me to become a person who is not lazy in any aspect of life. Renew my passion for sales. Renew my passion for helping others. Renew my passion for you.

In Jesus' name,
Amen.

MAKE OPPORTUNITIES HAPPEN

Find Opportunities to Pray

The death of a career in sales comes when the professional no longer looks for prospects. Whether you are recruiting for junior workers or looking for your next sale, you must seize every opportunity to prospect. Unless you are in a highly specialized field, you can find prospects everywhere. You must find a way to turn average conversations into consumer opportunities. When you believe in what you are doing, you will naturally brag about the advantages of your products.

If you have the greatest product the world has never seen, what good is the product? I have a rule that I try to stick to as a pastor. If I am paying someone for their time and expertise, I am entitled to talk to them briefly about spiritual matters. Now understand, I don't throw up on them (telling too much and taking too long to tell it). However,

I will explore spiritual things with them. I have been able to minister to and pray for many people by utilizing this principle. If you are paying someone for their services, they in turn should be willing to listen to you tell about your product. Prospecting is merely probing to find ways to help someone else with your products.

Ask questions that cause people to want to talk to you. Here are two examples of questions that you can tailor to your needs. "If there was a product that could benefit you more than what you currently own, would you want to know about it?" "Would you be disappointed if I had a product that could potentially save you a lot of money and I didn't tell you about it?"

I imagine God feels like a frustrated sales manager trying to motivate associates to use the tools provided for them. You can pray anywhere, anytime, about anything. God must think, "Why don't you just do it? Pray! Don't you like the rewards of doing what I have asked you? Don't you like the peace and comfort of knowing you can unload on me?"

God is so patient. He wants you to come to the place in your life where a conversation with Him is as natural as eating and breathing. You don't have to think about talking to a friend when he or she is right beside you, do you? Why is talking to God so difficult? Just as the children's song says, "You've got a friend in me," God is trying to convince you of his friendship. He is a friend willing to listen to you. You can spend your day walking and talking with God or you can go it alone. It is up to you. God's desire, however, is to spend time with you. He wants to spend time with you because He loves you.

God promises that if you will call on him he will answer you and show you great and unsearchable things that you do not know. Memorize Jeremiah 33:3, fondly known as God's phone number: *Call to me and I will answer you and tell you great and unsearchable things you do not know.*

God desires a conversation with you. Will you oblige him? He promises to show you things that are greater than you can imagine right now. The pledge is to show you unsearchable things that will benefit you. God's promises are sure. When he says He will do something, He will do it. You can count on God. He is reliable 100 percent of the time.

What kind of things does God want you to talk about in prayer? The answer is simple, everything. He wants you to experience a personal relationship with Him. He desires to hear you spill your guts! Your conversation should cover joys, sorrows, needs, concerns, wants and dreams. Do not be selfish! Pray for yourself, but do not forget to pray for others as well. "Any concern too small to be turned into prayer, is too small to be made into a burden," said Corrie Ten Boom. Nothing is too small or too big for God.

Many of the things we worry about are not concerns at all. Jesus reminded us that if the Father takes care of the birds and the flowers, he takes greater care of his children. He loves you and wants you to seek first his kingdom. He wants you to know his righteousness. When you talk to God about these needs, it gives him the opportunity to remind you that he is already providing for these things.

THE PRAYING SALES REP

My father-in-law, Jim, made one of the greatest statements of faith in God I have heard. He was going through the rigors of being terminated from a job he had been doing for over twenty years. We were at lunch with a friend of his and discussing the situation when Jim said, "Well, I'm not really concerned about it because God's got the problem now!"

"God's got the problem" is a powerful statement of faith. Our problems are God's problems. He wants to show you his glory in every situation. Think of Moses and Pharaoh, Joseph and his brothers, Daniel and the lion's den, all of them had tremendous problems. Still, at the same time, it was God's problem too. God has been faithful in the past, he is faithful in the present, and he will be faithful in the future. You can trust God.

When you turn to God in prayer, realize you are not providing Him with new information. God does not need your information. You need his. The Bible says that God already knows the intentions behind your thoughts and actions. Prayer is a conversation for your benefit. Kierkagaard wrote, "Prayer does not change God, but it changes him who prays."

The creator of the universe is willing to give his ear to your every word. To fail to seize every opportunity to pray is foolish. Utilizing the tool of prayer is essential to your walk with God. What good is a tool that is never used? Seize every opportunity you can to communicate with God today.

MAKE OPPORTUNITIES HAPPEN

Prayer Principle
Find Opportunities to Pray

Dear Jesus,

Help me to see and seize the opportunities you provide each day to help others with my products. I want to help others so that I can provide for their needs and the needs of my family. Lord, at the same time, help me to see that everything I go through today is an opportunity to pray. Let me see the needs of others, my personal needs, and even the concerns of strangers. I want to see you at work in my world.

In Jesus' name,
Amen.

POWER PRINCIPLE FOUR

HONESTY

Get Honest With God

Honesty in sales creates an environment for multiple sales. People award their business to companies and sales associates they deem as trustworthy. Franklin Roosevelt said, "Confidence . . .thrives on honesty, on honor, on the sacredness of obligations, on faithful protection and on unselfish performance. Without them it cannot live." Customer satisfaction is about service. Customers return because of integrity and trust.

The problem comes when sales associates are less than honest. "Honesty is the best policy," said Mark Twain, "when there is money in it." In your job, would you be a little less than honest if it would benefit you financially? Greed is an ugly monster seeking a willing accomplice in human form. Greed suggests to normally honest people that any means to financial success and power is okay. Besides, who is going to know?

Mary Kay Ash said, "Honesty is the cornerstone of all success, without which confidence and ability to perform shall cease to exist." Without your personal commitment to honesty, you will not create an atmosphere of confidence in your business. Without your personal commitment to honesty, you will not be able to continue to perform your job. Why? Because eventually your customers will go to someone else for your product.

When you or your associates are not honest, everyone's reputation is at risk. The name Enron will be forever linked with scandal. The words of Richard Nixon, "I am not a crook," will always be questioned. Bill Clinton's, "I did not have sexual relations with that woman," will be replayed over and over. When anyone is less than honest, sooner or later, that one will be hurt. Your reputation is too important to be linked with dishonest associates or practices.

Honesty is a vital link to our prayer lives. We must come to the place where we are honest about ourselves. An honest evaluation of your life will open you up to the ministry of the Holy Spirit. Do you have a hard time admitting your weaknesses? Why most people cannot admit weaknesses is because it makes them feel vulnerable. Here is a little secret, God already knows your weaknesses. God already knows what you need, but He has determined that you should ask for your needs in prayer. Remember this line of the Lord's Prayer, "Give us this day our daily bread." It is a prayer of honesty. God I am dependant upon your grace for even the basic needs of my life. Thank you for providing for me.

HONESTY

When you say, "God, I need you," you are as honest as a person can be. You declare your lack of personal ability when you have a need for God. You declare your dependence on your creator. You declare your trust that he cares about you. "God, I need you" is really your declaration of dependence. When you realize that you cannot make it in this world alone, then you are ready to come to life.

Not too long ago a politician was making a speech in which he declared, "Religion is just a crutch for weak-minded people." I have never met a person who was not weak-minded. The more self-sufficient one is, the more weak-minded one becomes. Jesus used a similar statement when he said, "It is not the well who need a doctor, but the sick." It is not the self-sufficient that need the Lord, it is the person who realizes that he or she needs help. The biggest hurdle to overcome is the recognition of the need for God.

God wants his children to come to him with an honest heart. He knows you inside and out. He wants the very best for you. You are uniquely equipped. If you are His child, He wants you to experience the abundant life He promised. Abundance may not come in the possession of worldly things but in the possession of heavenly things.

Even in our sorrows, God chooses to use us to our full potential. One of my Sunday school teachers from childhood was in the hospital dying of cancer. I was so upset. She was such a faithful Christian. I expressed to her my frustration over God allowing her to be sick. I will never forget what that faithful believer said. "If I was not sick, I wouldn't get to minister to all these doctors, nurses, and other people in the hospital." This sweet woman lived what Jesus said, "Father, your will be done."

Jesus was on his way to Jerusalem to be crucified when he passed through Jericho. As he was going out of the town, some beggars began to call out to him. Mark focuses on one of the blind beggars. His name was Bartimaeus. When Bartimaeus heard it was Jesus, he began to scream, "Jesus, Son of David, have mercy on me!" Bartimaeus persisted in calling even when the people around him tried to silence his cries. He called out again, "Jesus, Son of David, have mercy on me." Jesus picked Bartimaeus' voice out of the crowd and called the blind beggar over to him. When the man approached, Jesus asked him a simple question, "What do you want me to do for you?" The beggar replied just as simply, "Master, I want to see." Because of his faith, Jesus healed the beggar in a way Bartimaeus could not have imagined. Jesus not only healed the man's eyes, but he healed his soul. Jesus' response to the request was, "Go, your faith has saved you." The word Jesus used means Bartimaeus received sight for his eyes and his heart. Because he believed Jesus was more than a mere man, Bartimaeus' life was forever changed.

What do you want Jesus to do for you? What do you need to have Jesus do in and through you? Have you heard people use the slang phrase, "Honest to God?" It is a shame our society has denigrated great phrases into common slang. It is time for you to get honest toward God. God is with you. He knows the truth about your life. He knows what you need. Jesus is asking you the same question he asked blind Bartimaeus, "What do you want me to do for you?"

Prayer Principle
Get Honest With God

Dear Jesus,

Thank you for your call to honesty. I beg you to help me be a person of the highest form of integrity. Allow my actions and words reflect to all the world, to my clients, to my family, to my friends that I am trustworthy. Thank you that you are completely trustworthy. Help my lack of faith.

In Jesus' name,
Amen.

YOU ARE YOUR BEST PRODUCT

Growth in Prayer is Equal to Your Effort

Your absolute best product in your portfolio is you! It does not matter if you are selling real estate or ice cream. You are your best asset. The real question is how effective is your best product? How can you improve your best product?

Personal production increases as your confidence grows. Determining your strengths and weaknesses are vitally important. To be successful as a sales professional, you must be confident in your initial conversation with new people. Research has shown that you have ten seconds to make a good first impression before the client rejects your message. If you have an engaging personality and can provide a benefit to the client, he or she will listen further. As you continue to describe your product, the client will expect you to be knowledgeable and forthcoming. When you ask for the sale, you have to create an atmosphere of trust and acceptance. Rarely will a potential client buy a product from you if he or she dislikes you.

You are a vital link to your success. Learn people skills. Learn clear and effective communication skills. Learn how to help the client want your product. You are responsible for selling you. Vince Lombardi said, "The price of success is hard work, dedication to the job at hand, and the determination that whether we win or lose, we have applied the best of ourselves to the task at hand." You cannot change what others do, but you can change what you do.

This same concept is applicable to prayer. You are only as good as you are. You only grow in your prayer life to the extent that you are willing to dedicate yourself to prayer. The only person who cannot pray effectively is the person who only prays occasionally.

Sometimes church leaders and laypersons worry that they do not pray eloquently enough when praying aloud. Why do people think this? Because we are competitive by nature. We compare ourselves to each other. Prayer is not a sport. You should seek to master you.

In martial arts, someone earns the title master, not because that one has mastered others, but because that one has mastered self. He or she has developed their individual skills to the highest level. You should compare your praying skills to yourself. Your prayer life generally mimics your personal development as a Christian.

In order to get better at praying, you must pray. Just do it. Start talking to the Lord. He wants you too. He is begging you to learn to communicate with Him. When can you start? Right now! Now is the time for you to begin to pray. Start by planning and scheduling a prayer time. Do not look for eloquent or special words. Use your words. You are the one who is speaking to God. When you speak from your heart, you please God.

Reading the prayers found in the Bible will help you to learn to pray. If you are looking for subjects to pray about, read the Bible. You will find people who pray because they have a need for physical healing. People in the Bible prayed for food when they were hungry. The death of a loved one brought many people to their knees to ask for comfort and guidance. Major life decisions weighed on the hearts of God's people, new jobs, careers, or moves. The desire to have children was a huge concern for Abraham. Satan's attacks drove Jesus to pray to the Father. People sought God's help in the choice of a mate for themselves or for others. The prayer needs of the Bible are the same as the needs of people today. Learn from their successes and mistakes in prayer.

If you want to become more comfortable praying aloud, then you must pray aloud. Start by doing it in a small group setting or with a prayer partner. Your prayer partner could be your spouse. If you have children or grandchildren, pray aloud with them. You will grow and they will never forget those special times. Praying aloud takes practice. Just as you were not completely comfortable and relaxed when you entered your first sales position, it is the same when you pray corporately for the first few times. After some mysterious period of time, you suddenly became very comfortable and knowledgeable in your chosen field. The same will happen when you engage in praying before others.

Do not fall into the trap of trying to impress others with your ability to communicate with God. Instead, try to impress the heart of God with your sincerity and desire to seek his will. God told the children of Israel that he sought their obedience over their sacrifices. Religious ritual does not touch the heart of God. You move God when you do the things he asks simply because you love and respect him. He does not want forced prayer. He wants natural, heartfelt prayer. He wants prayers that are not contrived but contrite.

I almost exploded the other day with pride. A huge spiritual transformation was occurring in my oldest son. He went upstairs to read the Bible on his own. He didn't tell me but I overheard him telling his brother. Instead of me reading the Bible to him, he now wants to read the Bible for himself. He is already very spiritually astute. Suddenly, he is taking a huge stride forward in knowing what God wants him to do. He has gone to the source for Christians — the Bible. I have watched him pray for others and help others but now he is helping himself. I couldn't be prouder. I know there will be ups and downs in his spiritual walk, but for the moment I am so pleased. I imagine my feelings are very God-like. When God sees us doing the right thing, he is so proud. He knows it may not last long or it may be the beginning of greater things. However, for the moment, he is proud.

Just as sales are dependant on you, your prayer life is dependant on you. Try to please God with your initiative of getting to know him. When you grow both spiritually and intellectually, your business life and your prayer life will grow. Growth is initiated by you!

Prayer Principle
Growth is Equal to Your Effort

Dear Jesus,

Help me today to become a person of personal growth. Help me to develop my skills and abilities to express effectively how I can help others with my products. I want to be the best you created me to be. Likewise, I want to be the best I can be as a person of prayer. Help me to stay in your Word, the Bible, so that I may pray within the scope of your expressed will. Help me not to be competitive in prayer but efficient so that the praise may belong to you.

In Jesus' name,
Amen.

POWER PRINCIPLE SIX

LOOK 'EM IN THE EYES

Approach God with Boldness and Respect

One positive habit that you can develop is to look the client in the eyes when you make an assertion. People do not trust people in sales. Clients are always looking for the catch. If you make an assertion or make a concession to the client, he or she will wonder why. Some people think all people in sales are selling snake oil.

The problem of trust is not the only reason to look them in the eyes. When you pay attention to someone, you are acknowledging his or her worth. You are saying to the client, of all the people around us, you are the most important. There is nothing worse than for you to talk to a client but let your gaze move all around the room. You are sending a negative signal. If you are in sales, the client is the most important person right now. Do not answer phones. Do not look at your watch multiple times. Don't check your computer. Your client is the focus of your attention. Remove all distractions that are under your control.

Be careful when you look people in the eyes, though. If it appears you are staring a hole through the client, he or she will quickly become uncomfortable. Without eye contact, your client will think you are nervous, insecure, or insincere. Maintain a proper balance.

Looking clients in the eye shows that you respect and want to know their needs. It is a matter of "minding your manners." It is proper and polite to do so. Besides the social implications, paying attention to your clients enhances your listening skills. When you listen carefully, you will be ready to respond to needs intelligently and efficiently. I have observed people in sales completely miss what the client said because the salesperson focused too much on their presentation. You ask questions to move and direct the presentation, not to regroup and attack.

This principle applies to prayer in two ways. First, know to whom you are praying. You are praying to God, not just anyone. Approach Him with the reverence and respect He deserves. "The goal of prayer is the ear of God," wrote E. M. Bounds. Don't allow your attitude to plug the ears of God.

One of the positives and negatives coming out of the 1960's was the emphasis on God as our friend. I absolutely believe God is our friend. However, I must understand that His ways are higher than my ways; his thoughts are deeper than my thoughts. Just as I have a horizontal relationship with God that I define as friendship, equally I have a vertical relationship with God where I bow to Him as Lord. You cannot compare His holiness to our holiness. You cannot compare His faithfulness to our faithfulness. He is all that we can imagine and much, much more. He is the Lord God Almighty.

If you are praying to hear yourself talk, buy a digital recorder. If you are praying to learn God's heart, then approach him with respect. In the Psalms, the Lord tells us that he will not tolerate anyone who has haughty eyes and a proud heart. God is approachable, but remember you are approaching the King on his throne. God is not a beggar in need of your resources. You are the one in need of his abundant resources.

The second way this principle applies to prayer is that we should remove distractions when praying. Some people have tried to tell me about their times of prayer while driving, hunting, fishing, shopping, etc. While I believe it is possible to pray in these environments, it is impossible to have an intense conversation with God here. Don't force God to compete for your attention. Deep seasons of prayer often found Jesus retreating to a lonely place. He cherished moments of solace, spending time with his Father in quiet places. If Jesus needed this kind of environment to converse with the Father, how much more do we need to remove ourselves from distractions?

If the head of your corporation wanted to spend time with you, you would jump at the chance. You would feel special. You would feel important. You would seize the opportunity because of the chances for promotion and getting an edge on the competition and other employees would be in your favor. If this was possible, you might learn something extra to enhance your ability to do your job.

THE PRAYING SALES REP

When the head of your corporation wants to speak, you listen. When this one wants you to respond, you carefully weigh your words. You present the best picture of you that is possible. You would not let your cell phone, television, radio, or some sporting event interrupt that conversation. Unless it was a major emergency, you would not even allow a family member to interfere with this opportunity. You need to approach God the same way.

Sometimes our problems become detrimental to prayer. Oswald Chambers reminded us, "To pray with our eyes on God, not on the difficulties." We can become so self-absorbed with problems that we miss how God is at work through the difficulties. Not all difficulties are there to harm us. Some difficulties are there to prove God's faithfulness. Friends could have easily led Job into a pity party after losing most of his family, fortune, and health. Instead, he resisted the temptation to blame God or to be self-absorbed. He knew God was at work and he persisted in having faith in Him. Even when some people questioned whether sin caused a man's blindness, Jesus taught them that God allowed the disease to show his glory.

Have your problems caused you to doubt God? Have needs caused you to take your eyes off God? If you face either of these problems, make an intentional change. Change your focus from blame to shame. Be ashamed that you doubted God's concern for you. Be ecstatic that he wants to restore you. God does not hold a grudge, he holds his children. In fact, he holds his children close when times are hard.

LOOK 'EM IN THE EYE

Look 'em in the eyes has a variety of meanings. A client looks into a salesperson's eyes to find honesty. A salesperson looks at a client to create trust. When we look into the eyes of God, we find love.

Prayer Principle
Approach God with Boldness and Respect

Dear Jesus,

I am sorry for the times that I choose to focus on the world or my problems and not see what you are trying to teach me. Help me to learn from you. In doing so, make me a better person so that I can learn to listen and meet the needs of the clients you allow me to serve. Correct my inattention, Lord, for your glory.

In Jesus' name,
Amen.

WATCH YOUR LANGUAGE

Prayer Begins with Your Initiative

When you are in sales, you learn a language that is unique to your industry. That's why there are Barron's Dictionaries for areas of sales such as investments or real estate. If everyone understood your market-specific terms and how to do what you do, your job would be pointless. People come to sales professionals for two reasons: 1) for what you know or have and 2) for what they do not know or have.

Everyone could sell their own house, but most choose to use a professional to guide the process and to bring potential buyers to the home. Everyone could do their own taxes, but most will not take the time to learn how to sort through the procedures of the IRS. Understand this principle. You know more than the customer does, so they pay you. You have what they want, so they are willing to give their money to you in exchange for your knowledge or product. What you are saying, without words, is, "I know more than you, so pay me!"

The challenge for the sales professional is two-fold. First, how do I describe my product without seeming cocky and arrogant? Second, how do I communicate the need for my services so that the client understands what I offer? You may get away with being smug in an upscale restaurant with such a reputation, but you will not get away with that kind of attitude at the client's kitchen table. If you do, the client will escort you to the door. You must learn to be engaging and inviting. The client must see you as someone who values them as a person. Do not talk down to the client. When you educate the client, you are inviting him or her to make a decision based on knowledge.

When you decide it is your personal privilege and honor to present your information to the client, you will gain a hearing. Your choice of words can put your client at ease. If you use a term that is unique to your industry or your industry uses a term uniquely, take the time to explain to the client what you mean. If you have been in sales very long, you will hear that a client's "no" does not mean "never." It usually means "not now" or "I need more information." If your goal is to get a sale, you will master this concept. Clients want information. It is your privilege to provide that information.

Your goal in prayer is important. Why are you praying? Are you simply trying to ease your mind with words? Do you want to get some things off your chest? Or, are you seeking to communicate with God? As a pastor, I have lost focus in my public prayers by not watching what I say. What I mean is I will turn my prayers into a sermon if I am not careful. The goal of praying is not to communicate with my audience; it is to communicate with God on behalf of my congregation. Prayer is not touching the hearts of people, but touching the heart of God.

God wants to hear your needs and then communicate his plan for your needs. Prayer is a give and take. It is a time to listen and a time to reply. Your goal should be to learn to listen to God more than you talk. God is the expert on prayer. You have two ears and one mouth, use them proportionally. If God is the one with the knowledge, your goal should be to learn as much as possible from him.

How much money have you spent on your education to do your job? If you added it up, it would probably shock you. How many books have you bought on your subject? How many newspapers have you perused to find articles about your products or company? How many seminars have you been to? What did it cost for professional licenses or associations? It is amazing what we will spend for knowledge. We spend a great deal of money for knowledge, yet spiritually all we have to do is ask for it. God tells us if we lack wisdom, all we have to do is ask for it. God wants to provide you with the keys to abundant life. You just need to spend time with him figuring out what he thinks abundant means. The best place for continuing education as a Christian is in the Bible. Spend time reading it. Absorbing it. Dwelling on it. Then pray an educated prayer.

Prayer is not a foreign language that takes years of hard work and consistency to master. However, prayer is a combination of hard work and consistency. Prayer is hard work because no one but you can make you do it. You have to get up in the morning to pray. You have to pause periodically during work to focus on God. When you choose to ask a blessing on your food, prayer happens at mealtime. You have to approach his throne with boldness. Prayer for others occurs because you decide it will happen. You pray at bedtime because you kneel down to pray. Prayer is up to you. The ball is in your court. You will be surprised how quickly your prayer life will grow when you begin to pray. Remember, prayers will not pray for you. You must pray a prayer.

Prayer is consistency. Your prayer life should be consistent with who you are. The words you use in prayer should consist of words common to you. Real prayer occurs when God hears from you. You do not have to use a special spiritual language. You do not have to sound like your spiritual heroes. You need to sound like you. True prayer is not trying to mimic the words of spiritual super heroes. True prayer is when your heart is in tune with God.

Consistency also derives from persistency. You must persist in your desire to pray. Spending time with God should happen every day. You do it, because you love it. You love it, because you love the one with whom you are spending time. Prayer is like sitting in the shade of a porch, drinking a glass of iced tea, having a long, intimate conversation with a dear friend. Sit back, relax, and enjoy.

Prayer Principle
Prayer Begins with Your Initiative

Dear Jesus,

Today I ask you to help me value the people you give me the privilege of serving. Thank you for giving me someone I can help. May I show them love, respect, and gratitude. At the same time, I want to tell you "Thank You." Thank you for listening to me. Thank you for loving me. Thank you for taking me from where I am and leading me to where you want me to be.

In Jesus' name,
Amen.

PRACTICE YOUR PRESENTATION

Pray at Every Opportunity God Provides

P ractice makes perfect. There is nothing worse than not knowing your information when making a presentation. It erodes your confidence. It makes you look unprofessional. The client is concerned that you are not providing him or her with the proper information. The bottom line is a lack of preparation damages the reputation of your company, your supervisor, and you. Trust takes hours of hard work to establish and a moment to destroy.

One method to enhance your presentation skills is to practice with a friend or family member. This person will know you are practicing and if you provide the opportunity for positive or negative criticism, you will show that you really respect and expect to receive this person's opinion. Often, during these practice times, a sale will occur because the friend or family member pays careful attention to you in order to provide the feedback you requested. If you ask for criticism, do not argue. You do not have to agree, but you should listen attentively. Make notes on what your friend tells you. Afterward, you can reflect on the person's input and determine your course of action.

A second way to enhance your presentation skills is to listen to different people in your company make a sales presentation. If you can pick up one detail from each presentation observed, you will soon find that your presentation becomes very polished. Don't try to imitate your co-worker. Instead, identify certain elements that you can incorporate in the way you do your presentation.

A third suggestion is to record your presentation. Most people are their own worst critic. If you can get to the point where you can tolerate listening to your presentation, you are probably doing better than you think. Video is the best media to use to record your presentation. By using video, you can analyze your gestures, posture, and eye contact. Your trainer or supervisor can also use this recording to give you a better analysis of your presentation. The trainer can take the time to rewind the presentation and reevaluate his or her suggestions.

The fourth suggestion is just do it. The more presentations you give the better you will become. You will develop a comfortable pace. You will become more effective at telling your story. You will become confident because you are seeing results, i.e. making sales. There is no substitute for just doing it.

These four suggestions work equally well with prayer. Praying aloud with a family member or friend helps you become comfortable in this situation. Praying for or with someone will allow you to get feedback on how effectively you communicated your thoughts. You need to practice praying aloud just to get comfortable hearing your voice. If you choose to pray with family, they will already know you are doing something you are not used to doing. Your efforts at getting closer to God will affect family members' lives. You will be a great inspiration to your children. Your spouse will grow closer to God or begin to think about God because of you. Praying with others will give you another outlet for ministry Prayer is not the least you can do for someone. It is the best you can do.

If you are trying to become comfortable praying in your worship services, you should come early and get used to hearing your voice in the sound system. Different sanctuaries and sound technicians make what you hear on the platform sound different. You need to be comfortable. Simply ask, if you know you are going to pray that day, if you can read a passage of scripture into the microphone to help you become comfortable with your surroundings. If you come early enough this should not be a problem for the musicians or the ministers with any last minute preparations they are doing.

You can pick up words or phrases from other people when they pray that might help you as you are learning. This is a perfectly correct manner of learning. Make sure you are not repeating someone else's words unless the words are truly expressing the desires of your heart. Do not develop one prayer as your standard public prayer. I have heard people pray the same prayer every time they have prayed publicly. This is a very childish way to pray. It is not communication with God. It is mouthing words without true thought. Even times of corporate prayer should be communication with God, not entertainment for the congregation. I have heard other people try to impress the congregation with their prayers. If the words you utter in prayer are not consistent with the way you communicate to other people, then you are trying to be an actor. You are not performing when the pastor invites you to pray. Your invitation is to communicate with God on behalf of the congregation. Read the prayers found in the Bible of corporate prayer. Model your prayers after these examples.

If your church has a video or audio of the worship service, you can review your public prayers. Do not overanalyze or criticize yourself. Honestly evaluate your effectiveness and strive to get better in one area at a time. Prayer is not about pretty words. It is about an acceptable heart. God desires obedience over sacrifice and ritual. God wants you to be yourself. Moses stuttered. Elisha was baldheaded. Paul was nearsighted. Yet God used them just as they were. God wants you to approach him as yourself, not an imposter. At the same time, strive to be the best you that is possible.

Finally, just do it. Start finding places that you can pray aloud. Go visit someone in the hospital, nursing home, or ministry center. Pray for people you meet. Sometimes God will lead you to pray silently; at other times, you will need to pray with that person. When someone asks you to pray for them, stop right then and pray with them for the particular need. That way you will not forget the need and you will have seized the opportunity to be a blessing. The more you pray, the better you will get. The more you pray, the more you will be blessed. Just do it.

Prayer Principle
Pray at Every Opportunity God Provides

Dear Jesus,

Help me to be an effective presenter of the materials my job provides. Will you help me to convey the passion I have for my products to my clients? Lord, teach me to be professional, courteous, and forthright. At the same time, help me to understand my weaknesses and seek to improve so I can represent you, my company, and myself in the best manner possible. Thank you for being patient with my prayer life. Help me to be comfortable but respectful in all that I express to you.

In Jesus' name,
Amen.

LISTEN THEN TALK

Pray at Every Opportunity God Provides

Have you heard the maxim: "You have two ears and one mouth, use them in proportion?" A common problem for people in sales is not listening to the customer. Your greatest ally can be your potential client. If you will learn to ask open-ended questions, you will allow the customer to tell you his or her needs. When you develop this technique, you can focus your presentation on what is important to the customer. By doing this you can make the best use of your client's time. If the client feels that you are concerned about his or her company, a sale is more likely to occur. Your goal is to make a sale, isn't it? To do so, you have to value the client's opinion and discern specific needs that you can meet.

Numerous books can help you with questions for the presentation and the close. One is Tom Hopkin's book, *How to Master the Art of Selling.* A classic book on closing a sale is Zig Ziglar's, *Secrets of Closing the Sale.* Both are particularly useful for developing listening skills. For instance, in Ziglar's book, he is talking to a car salesman about a new Cadillac. When the salesman told him the price, Ziglar expressed shock at the figure. The salesman did not become defensive. He did not go on the offensive. He simply asked for more information with a strategic question, "Mr. Ziglar, is it too much?"

If you ask the right questions, you will get the right answers. The key is to learn how to ask questions for more information. With the right questions, you will get to know the needs and desires of your client. You should not ask questions without a purpose, instead ask questions to direct and control the conversation.

A client will describe fears of the product, if you will listen. He or she will tell you why the timing is not right to buy your product at this time. If you listen, you will learn what you can and cannot overcome by a good sales presentation. You simply cannot overcome objections if the objection is based on a relationship with someone that the client absolutely trusts. Find out how to use the information the client gives you to your advantage. Nevertheless, you will never use the information if you do not listen.

When you are talking to God, you should apply the same maxim, use your ears and mouth proportionally. Many believers make the mistake of only speaking to God and never listening. A basic definition of prayer is a conversation with God. A conversation, however, assumes two parties are participating.

LISTEN THEN TALK

Does God want you to talk to him? Definitely, he does. He desires for you to let your request be known to him. The Bible says, through Jesus, we can boldly approach the throne of God. We need no one to go before God for us. Why is this? It is because Jesus provided us with direct access to the Father. Jesus said, "Ask and it will be given to you, seek and you will find, knock and the door will be open to you."

The term asking is balanced in scripture with the term listening. The Father has called us to listen to Jesus. At the Mount of Transfiguration God said, "This is my Son. Listen to him!" God expects us to be good listeners. His Son has something important to say. Jesus' words were important to his world, they are important to our world, and they are important to you!

Jesus reminded his followers numerous times to listen to his parables. Not only were the disciples to listen but they were to listen carefully. Jesus knew it was important for the disciples to hear his message correctly. In fact, Jesus knows it is important for you to hear his message correctly.

We must always be ready to listen carefully when God speaks. You might ask how he speaks. He speaks through the recorded words of the Bible. The Bible is God-breathed or God-directed. God, through the means and words of select individuals, delivered and gave life to His perfect Word. Jesus acknowledged the Scriptures of his day as God's Word. The New Testament saints viewed the Old Testament in the same way, as nothing less than God's Word. The Bible is not just a good book. It is the Book. The Bible is God-speak. It is God making sure we hear clearly.

THE PRAYING SALES REP

The second way we hear from God is in our hearts. When we pray and listen, we will hear God impressing his message on our hearts through His Spirit. You might say that sounds extremely subjective. It is subjective. It is subject to you listening correctly. However, the balance to this subjectivism is the Bible. If what you hear does not measure up with what the Bible says, you can be sure what you heard is not from God. God does not contradict himself. He will not change what he has already said. When he speaks through his Spirit who resides in you, he speaks the consistent Word of God. He is not revealing new things. He is retelling old things. He is sharing old things in a fresh way to you.

When praying, it is good to get to the place of quiet listening. Do not allow Satan to interfere with your prayer time by way of distractions. Eliminate and investigate. Eliminate things that would distract you from hearing God's Word. Investigate the things that you hear God saying. You need to hear a clear word from God.

Experts say we spend the first three or four years of a child's life teaching him to walk and to talk. Then we spend the next twenty trying to get him to sit down and shut up. You must learn this in prayer. In very blunt terms, you must sit down, shut up, and listen. In order to do so, you must be still and know that he is God.

Prayer Principle
Carefully Listen to God through Prayer

Dear Jesus,

I want to learn and hear from you. I pledge to pay attention to your instruction in the Bible in order to pray and hear clearly. Help me to become the kind of person who listens to people. Help me to practice listening to people in everyday conversation, so I might become a more effective sales representative.

In Jesus' name,
Amen.

TIME MANAGEMENT

Protect Your Prayer Time at All Costs

Theft is a huge problem in sales. However, it is preventable. When you enact a loss prevention strategy, you will become profitable. What is the number one item that is stolen in sales? Your time. You must create a strategy to quit losing it. Making the best use of your time makes you money! Waste time and you will lose money.

What are some activities that steal your time? One thing that steals your time is the unnecessary use of great tools. The telephone has cost you hundreds or possibly thousands of dollars. The telephone is a tool. It does not make money. It does not sell your product. You do. The computer is another great tool that people in sales abuse. If you are reading ten newspapers per day, just to see the same news, it is a waste of your time. You do not need to know the weather in Hackensack until it makes you money. Unless your job entails spending hours on the computer, you need to limit computer usage to what is necessary. A second thief is the lack of priorities. What should I be doing now? Without a strategy for the day, you will kill many hours but make no money. What enhances my skills or creates a sale? Do those activities. Find out what successful people in your line of sales do, and then do that. Find the most successful person in your office and do the things that person does. The third thief that shows up is the unexpected guest. These people want you to spend all your time with them. Do you want to eat an early lunch today? Can you show me how the new printer works? Today would be a great day to get in an extra round of golf. If you open the door, this guest will rob you of your time.

A clean desk is a sign of a sick mind. Someone has shared this proverb with you at sometime. Actually, statistics say that the most productive people work from clean desks. A cluttered desk is a sign of unfinished work. Unfinished work leads to desk stress and a lack of productivity. The inability to say no and procrastination go hand-in-hand with the loss of time. If every time someone asks you to help, to do some menial task, or to explain something and you stop to do it, you will lose precious time. Remember you can never reclaim wasted time. Organization and the ability to see a task through to the end are important aspects of sales.

In order to be productive, you should develop a time management strategy. A way to start is by PADing your time. P: Plan. Create a plan for your day and stick to it. If you do not know where you are going, any road will get you there. Create a plan to go somewhere today, and stick to it. You should know which tasks must be accomplished. Make a list of priorities. Start with the tasks you must finish, and then list secondary tasks, etc. A: Analyze. Analyze where you are spending your time. This task should not take a lot of your time. Open your calendar and examine the last two months or even two weeks. A quick overview should help you to see where you have time that you could spend more productively. When you look at where you are wasting time, you move to D: Define. Define your objectives. Defining objectives is more than just creating a plan. It is creating a plan with a purpose. You are refining the plan to be the most productive. There may be two tasks that are important, but which of the two is most important and why.

Success follows strategy. Rarely will someone stumble on success. Usually one will work long and hard to become successful. I had a conversation with a very successful heart surgeon. He told me when he established his first practice his receptionist was netting more income than he was. However, with a lot of hard work, he stuck with his plan and now is very successful. When you define what you must accomplish every day then you can answer two other questions. Where am I wasting time? And, how am I going to turn that wasted time into a productive action? When you PAD your time, you will begin to take control of your day. If you do not know what you are going to do daily, you are creating a plan to fail. Many people fail in sales because they cannot handle the freedom a career in sales affords.

The same activities rob us from the blessing of a productive prayer life. When your time manages you instead of you managing your time, you will never make time for prayer. You must organize your time, removing the clutter, to spend quality time with your heavenly Father. When you prioritize your life, you will spend quantity time with the Father. We should seek to spend more time with the Lord. If you truly believe he has a plan for your life, you need to start listening to him.

PADing works for prayer, too. P: Create a plan to have a prayer time. Schedule it, prioritize it, and do not let anything rearrange it. You are only successful in your prayer life when you are willing to work the plan. A: Analyze your prayer time. How often do you pray? When do you pray best? When do you need prayer most during your day? What is interrupting your prayer time? What can you do to stop the distractions? D: Define your objectives. Why do you want to pray? What benefit is prayer for you? What do you need to discuss with God? Clarifying questions will help you stay on track in your prayer time.

You must manage you prayer time or something will come up to distract you from your objectives. Take control. It is up to you whether or not you become a willing accomplice in the theft of your time.

Prayer Principle
Protect Your Prayer Time at All Costs

Dear Jesus,

Your Word tells me to do all things as if I am doing them for you. Help me to give you my job as a witness of my commitment to you. I ask you to correct me when I am so easily distracted. Especially, correct me when I allow distractions to hinder me from spending time with you. May I prioritize and protect my time to a productive citizen of the Kingdom of God.

In Jesus' name,
Amen.

POWER PRINCIPLE ELEVEN

KEEP YOUR PRESENTATION FRESH

AND CURRENT

Do Not Allow Your Prayer Life to Stagnate

Everyone likes the comfortable over the uncomfortable. If variety is the spice of life, why do we hate change so much? We like to know what is ahead rather than being surprised by the future. Why do people fear death? Their fear comes from the unknown. How am I going to die? What happens when I die? Instead of looking forward to death as most religions teach, we dislike even talking about the subject. Death is radically different from our comfortable living.

Why do you practice sales presentations repeatedly? You want to be comfortable. You want to know your material well. You want to look professional. However, what do you think will happen to the quality of your presentation if you do not create a degree of variety? You will become bored with your own presentation if it never changes. You will loathe having to present your material. If you are bored, you are boring your client.

The definition of a rut is a grave with both ends kicked out. If you do not create variety in your work, you will die. Your sales career depends on your ability to incorporate cheerleading, teaching, administration, service, closing and timing into a balanced relationship. If you focus exclusively on one aspect, you will be in a rut and die. You cannot master just part of your job; you must master the whole thing. Could you imaging an ophthalmologist telling you, "I can administer the eye examine, but I can't tell you if you need glasses." Learn all of the vital aspects of your particular avenue of sales.

The ability to vary your presentation helps you to analyze and address your client's needs. The client may or may not know how your product will help his or her company. However, in the warm-up period of your presentation, you can discover information that will help you whet your client's appetite for your product. Listen attentively. If you are listening and asking proper questions, you can vary your presentation to engage and grab the attention of your client.

For instance, if you are selling financial products and the client tells you his father services his property and casualty insurance, you ought to know you are not going to get that block of business. You will not overcome the emotional attachment of a client and a father. If you are wise, you will mention that you might be able to save him some money in that area, but that you have another product that will benefit the client right now. By making a statement about insurance, you are keeping open the possibility; however, you definitely have something else that will interest the client. You might even say, "I am sure your father is doing a wonderful job for you, but if I could save you a substantial amount of money, would you be interested?" If you are stuck in the same old routine, you cannot or will not change your presentation. You must be ready to redirect the conversation immediately. If you are not flexible, you will lose business. Large companies change their marketing strategy based on the needs of clients. You must be willing to change your presentation also to meet the needs of a particular client.

Just like a sales presentation, your prayer life can stagnate. If every conversation you have with God is the same, you will soon get tired of praying. Unless you are a child, you should not pray repetitious prayers. God says he does not hear you because of your words. He hears you because of your heart. Talk to God just as you would anyone else that you highly respect.

One way to add variety to your prayer time is to add songs to your prayers. Songs evoke strong emotions and touch your life. Have you ever had a song stuck in your head? How difficult is it to forget it? If you are like me, sometimes that is nearly impossible. I will hear a tune all day.

Songs put words into your mouth that you otherwise might not be able to express. The Bible says when you do not know how to pray as you should, the Holy Spirit makes intercession for you. However, you should strive to be able to express to God what is on your heart. Songs can help you vocalize what you would like to tell God.

Recently, I watched victims of a hurricane wipe away rivers of tears during a church service when they sang songs that were special to them. Why did a song evoke such strong emotions? I think it is because we get so caught up in our hurts, pains, or fears that we forget the words that need to come out of our mouths to God. Then we hear a song that reminds of the steadfast love of God, his amazing grace, or his nearness and we subconsciously think, "I want to say that to God." When this happens, the tears flow and God begins to bring us healing.

The emotions that stir in your heart when you hear music, can aid your prayer time. Do certain songs make you cry, laugh, or dance? Enjoy the outbursts at the appropriate time and place. Prayer does not have to be a very quiet time. It can be joyful. All of your emotions need to be a part of your prayer time. God made you the emotional being that you are. Some of you express your emotions openly, others express emotions privately. No matter which end of the spectrum you fit into, you need to become completely involved in prayer.

Passages of scripture you read or memorize can transform your prayer life. The Bible directs your prayer to the heart of God. He spoke it. Sermons. Devotions. Blogs. Daily life. Circumstances. Triumphs. Tragedies. All of these create opportunities for variety in prayer.

C. S. Lewis said, "God sometimes seems to speak to us most intimately when he catches us, as it were, off our guard." When you pray, don't be intimidated by the intimacy of prayer. Do not be surprised when God speaks loudly or softly in your heart. He loves you. He wants to communicate with you. Allow variety to become normal in your prayer times.

Prayer Principle
Do Not Allow Your Prayer Life to Stagnate

Dear Jesus,

Thank you for giving me the ability to be a person who can think and act with both wisdom and emotion. Help my career be fresh not for my sake only but for the countless clients I can help with the tools provided to me. God, help my prayer life not become repetitive and bland. May I be moved by the emotions and circumstances of daily life to come before your throne with rejoicing, thanksgiving, and needs.

In Jesus' name,
Amen.

EDUCATE YOUR CLIENTS

Enhance Your Prayer Time

Most consumers do not view sales people's opinions as authoritative on their industry. Granted, people think you know your product. However, they think you know it to make a buck. One way to show the value in the service you are providing is to quote independent sources. You can find quotes to support your products in national magazines, industry resources, and national consumer research groups. If you can find someone other than your company touting the benefits of what you do, you have found proof for your argument.

If you are successful in sales, you generally have other folks working for you. The more successful you are, the more those close to you in your office will accept what you say without questioning you. You can see the problem forming. Larry Burkett said, "Perhaps nothing in our society is more needed for those in positions of authority than accountability. Too often those with authority are able (and willing) to surround themselves with people who support their decisions without question." Make sure that what you say is solid, fact-supported information. Just because something works does not make it right.

If you think that a consumer will accept what you say without question, then you are delusional. A good consumer wants you to work for the sale. The consumer also wants you to educate him or her. If you prove your point through a process of education, the consumer will reward you with his or her business. Don't take the act of a consumer offering you their money lightly. That is a moment of trust. Once you have gained the client's trust, do not lose it.

Your level of service should go up once you have someone's money. Some people in sales think that once you get the sale your job is finished. In reality, the education process is just beginning. Periodically make contact to reassure the client that they made the right decision. You can send them independent articles that review their need or purchase, info on your company that will create confidence, or an offer to reevaluate their needs with your latest products. Quotes by other experts are more powerful than the price of a good product. You enhance the value of your service by offering the client continuing education. This kind of material has the potential to reward you with future business. The little extras offer what a client looks for in a company, service after the sale.

EDUCATE YOUR CLIENTS

When you pray, quotes have the potential to reward you as well. What kind of quote am I proposing? The quotation of Scripture as a source for prayer will transform you. The Bible is an unlimited resource of prayer topics. When your prayer life becomes dry, read. Passages of scripture provide you with several things. First, you can find promises to claim. God has many promises for you to discover, but before you can strike oil, you have to pick up a shovel. Start digging by reading the Bible.

Second, you can find sin to confess. God is always trying to heighten your sense of character. Throughout the Bible, you will find ways to improve who you are. In my life, God started with the big things, sin that stood out to others. My language began to change. The places I hung out needed changing. Actions that I took needed refining. Outward attitudes toward people had to change dramatically. As I started growing in the Lord, He began to weed out the smaller things. I needed to learn to trust Him instead of me. The will and desire to listen to God was developed. God started convicting me of thoughts and attitudes. It finally struck me; God is interested in refining the things that only He and I see. It is like planting a garden. You must start with turning the soil before you can harvest the crop.

Third, you can find ways to minister to others. Prayer is not just about you. Talk to God about the ways he wants you to give to your community. A disciple is never really a disciple, until he or she is making disciples. Your prayer time should consist of finding scriptures that will help you train others. Pick up God's Word and ask him to show you verses to help you help others. Jesus told his disciples,

"If you want to be great in the kingdom of God become servants of all people."

Devotional works, such as Oswald Chambers', *My Utmost for His Highest*, are a great source to help you utilize scriptures for prayer. Your church probably offers various publications of a devotional nature. Utilize these to enhance your prayers. Many free internet devotionals can help you too. A search for devotionals will lead you to these sites. You need to work as hard to find your voice in prayer as you do to find a client you can help.

What is the power in scripture? First, the Bible informs you as to how God thinks. If you learn how God thinks, then you can pray effectively. If you believe God created you in his image, then you should seek to train your mind to think the way God thinks. Effectual prayer avails much, according to book of James. Prayer becomes effectual when you focus your prayers through the Word of God. Second, the Bible equips you for spiritual warfare in prayer. Prayer is a battle. Satan does not want you to pray. God loves when you do. Satan does not want a Christian to experience intimacy with God. God wants you to know Him personally. Satan wants you to experience God sporadically and superficially. God wants you to be with him always. When you learn this lesson, you will never want to go back to mediocrity. You will want more. Imagine, if Jesus needed to use scripture when resisting the arrows of Satan how much more do you need to know the scriptures.

Prayer Principle
Use the Bible and Other Materials to Enhance Your Prayer Time

Dear Jesus,

Help me to be great in your kingdom by serving others. I want to be the best that I can become in my business. Direct me to materials, resources, and people to serve the most people I can. In my prayer life, may I see the value and direction your Word brings to all aspects of life. Help me to stay current with you.

In Jesus' name,
Amen.

LEARN TO SAY, THANK YOU

Show Your Thanks to God by Your Actions

It will cost you less to keep a customer than to find a new one. According to the United States Office of Consumer Affairs, a customer, who is dissatisfied, tells between 10 and 20 associates about their dissatisfaction. Another startling statistic is that it costs approximately five times more to gain the trust of a new client than to retain a loyal customer. If a customer loses trust in your company, 93 percent will never tell you why. These former customers will simply give their business to someone else. However, 95 percent of customers with complaints will come back if you take care of their problems and offer excellent service.

One of the worst things a representative can do is to act as if the customer works for the representative, instead of vice versa. Clients need to know you appreciate the opportunity to service their needs. When clients want to spend their money on your services, or even explore the possibility, you should acknowledge your appreciation. You should never take customer appreciation lightly.

To retain customers, a car dealer in a small market offered a customer appreciation night. Mack Grubbs would have his auto shop cleared out, spit shined, and loaded with simple games for the customers who bought a new vehicle in the last year. The games tempted both adults and children. Everyone won each game played. Prizes included hats, pens, oil changes, coupons to fast food restaurants, and many other giveaways. Barbeque grills supplied a steady stream of hot dogs and hamburgers. Soft drinks cooled off customers on the hot summer nights. After all these rewards, each family received a large package of fresh sausage links when they departed. People loved it. They were special. No one else in town said thank you like Mack.

Tell your customers how important they are to you. It is vitally important to your business. From the time a customer walks on your premises, until the time they leave, you should make them feel like you have been waiting all day to help them. I have been in stores where no one greeted me, no one asked if they could help, and no one asked for a sale. So what do you think I did? I left and gave my money to someone else.

New Orleans is famous for having rude salespeople. At the grocery stores, when I was in seminary, it was common to go through the checkout line, have everything scanned, and the clerk would simply hold out his or her hand without telling you how much the total was. I must admit, that just chaps my hide. The first time this grocery game happened, it caught me off guard and I fell into the trap of forking over the dollars. The next time was a different story. When I went through the line, the girl stuck out her hand and I just stood there. She waited and I waited. You know the maxim, "The first one to speak loses." After a minute, she finally said, "Sir that will be $10.95." Of course, I had to continue the game by saying, "I'm sorry, what did you say?" So, the girl had to repeat it. I figured it was good practice for her and it sure pleased me. I then proceeded to count out my money and said, "I am so sorry, I forgot the amount. What was the price again?" I am quite sure she was glad when I left. However, I felt I had at least broken even in the negotiation of grocery store checkout.

In prayer, we need to tell God thank you. Remember it is one thing to say thank you. It is quite another thing to show thanks. When you pray you should thank God for the simple things. You can thank God for life, breath, and waking you up today. Once you thank him for your life, you should live it to prove your thanks. Your life should be a reflection of God's image in you. You show thanks by living as he created you to live. You can say thank you to God for providing food and water. Afterwards, share some of your food with one less fortunate. If you look on the labels of several staple items, like bottled water, it contains a serving for two. The serving is enough for you and someone else. It also provides a ministry opportunity through Jesus' name.

Another simple prayer of thanks is for your family. When you pray for your family, reflect on how you are treating those that you love. Do you spend enough time with your spouse or children? Are you as interested in their personal development as you are in your own success? Why do you work the way you do? Is it to help your family or is it to fulfill personal goals? Would your family be better off with fewer things and more of you?

I try to cherish every moment with my children. I have realized that I can never have their younger years back. I love to hear their questions of why, the how, and the misspoken words. I don't get to participate in these if I'm out of balance with work and family. Sure, the silliness can be a bit much sometimes. However, I can promise you, I will miss those things the most when they are older and do not do them. The other day my son was willing to sit in the chair with me and let me hold him for just a moment. Those days are becoming fewer and farther between, because he is becoming a little man. I wish I would have know a few days before he quit being my little boy. I would have played even more kid games. I would have taken a few days off. Those days are more important than any spent in the office. Thank the Lord for your family.

It is essential to say thank you to your loyal customers. You should also show your thanks for the customers' continued support of your business. You have invested too much time, energy, and money to lose a customer. It is more important, however, to show your appreciation to God. God has invested too much time, energy, and heavenly money in you for you to forget him.

LEARN TO SAY, THANK YOU

Prayer Principle
Show Your Thanks to God by Your Actions

Dear Jesus,

I am so consumed with success some days that I forget how true success looks. Help me to appreciate my clients more. My family more. My time with You more. May I not just say thank you. Help me to live in such a way as to show my thanks for every opportunity.

In Jesus' name,
Amen.

MAKE YOUR CLIENT FEEL

APPRECIATED

Praise God for All the Blessings of Life

How well you know your client will determine to what extent this principle works. A business owner in a town I pastored made a lasting impression on me. When I moved into town, the local newspaper ran an article welcoming the new pastor. This owner was not a member of the new church and he did not do business with the church. He just went out of his way to send me a laminated copy of the article and to welcome me to town. I immediately sent him a note to say thank you. Then I told everyone about his kindness. I even used his act of kindness as a sermon illustration. His thoughtfulness resulted in thousands of dollars of free advertising. Throughout the time I lived in the town, I would receive additional laminated articles from him when the church or my kids were in the newspaper. His simple scanning of the newspaper and having a secretary send out articles had a huge return on a very small investment.

How can a business brag on clients if you do not have personal interaction with them or they are not in the public eye? Applebee's, a chain restaurant, made my kids feel great every year when they were young. One day while we were in the restaurant, my children asked to sign up for the kids club. We did and for multiple years the kids received birthday wishes from Applebee's. Each one received free meals and I paid for at least two adult portions. What a great marketing tool. The restaurant already knows I like them. I let my kids give them personal information. Then they use my kids to force me into another visit to the restaurant that I might not have made otherwise. I leave the restaurant feeling great because my kids got a meal free and I think I saved money. When in actuality, I spent more money than I normally would have.

Another small business in New Orleans, a toy store, sent the kids $10 in store money for their birthday. So guess where I went to spend an additional $20 or $30 on toys. Almost every business collects birthday information. A simple card to mark another milestone in life would be a way to brag on your clients.

If you want to be successful in sales, whether it is retail or direct marketing, you must be willing to do what other people are unwilling to do. Knowing your clients and bragging on their successes is not what most people in sales do. You can gain a tremendous advantage by taking the time to celebrate life events with your clients.

MAKE YOUR CLIENT FEEL APPRECIATED

The word praise comes from a Latin word that means price or value. When you praise someone, you are placing a price or value on their worth. When you praise God, you are telling him how valuable your relationship with him is. Praise is a simple act of bragging on the fact that God knows you, he provides for you, and he cares for you. As you offer praise to God, you are practicing for your life in heaven. The Bible says that the angels constantly cry out the praise of God before his throne. They teach us how to show God's value to him and to all the world.

What is God's value to you? When you begin to construct your answer to this question, you will begin to find ways to praise God. When you think of his creative powers, you can identify reasons to praise him. Do you like the trees, the sky, the sea, or the mountains? These are all reasons to praise him. An old chorus reminds us to, "Love him in the morning when you see the sun arising, love him in the evening 'cause he's brought you through the day." David used all that is in the heavens and all that is on the earth to describe how we should praise him. "Let the heavens rejoice and the earth be glad. Let the seas and all that are in it be filled with his praise." All of God's majesty should drive those who recognize his works and worth to sing his praises.

The redemptive work of Jesus is a huge reason to praise God. God has always shown his redeeming nature. From the beginning with Adam and Eve to the cross of Christ, we see God reaching out to his creation to say, "I love you and I will fix your brokenness." God loves you enough to accept you with all your mistakes and invest in all your potential.

THE PRAYING SALES REP

Have you thanked God for his forgiveness and his promise of heaven for you? Have you considered praising him for the salvation of family members? I began to pray for the salvation of my children from the moment we knew my wife was pregnant. I would put my hand on my wife's growing baby bump and pray for the child's safety and for my child to grow up to be a great man or woman of God. I would thank God that He who began a good work in this child would be faithful to complete the task. I thanked God that he fearfully and wonderfully made my children with his own hands. I praised him that before I knew my children, God knew them individually.

If you will notice the times in the Bible that people or angels praise God, you will discover ways to brag on God. There are prayers in the Bible of thanks for wives and children. God receives praise for his protection of Israel and the people of the nation. When you have food to eat, you should thank him. When you are suffering afflictions, you should praise God because afflictions lead to hope. God loves you, he is wise, and he is concerned about you. These things and so many others are right before your eyes. Seize every opportunity to praise others and the Lord. Will you commit to bragging on God, at least once, today?

Prayer Principle
Praise God for All the Blessings of Life

Dear Jesus,

Today, I simply and sincerely want to say "Thank You." I want to give you praise for everything in my life.

In Jesus' name,
Amen.

HELP PEOPLE ACHIEVE

THEIR DREAMS

Prayer is a Way to Help Others

"You can get whatever you want in this world, as long as you help enough other people get what they want," said Zig Ziglar. His principle is one of the greatest summations of how to achieve personal success. To be successful in almost any endeavor, you must find a way to meet others' needs. If you sell cars, you must find the car that your client wants. If you help people with financial products, you must show your clients how your product will meet their financial needs. If you work in retail, you must find the clothing, jewelry, or appliance your shopper wants.

People all have dreams. The problem with dreams is that as many people get older they quit chasing dreams to settle for something less. If you ever quit having dreams and believing you can achieve them, you will settle for less than what you might be capable of accomplishing. It is better to have tried and failed than to fail to try. Chances are you will not have success without a host of failures. There is a saying, "If you are knocked down seven times, you must get up eight." Your job in sales is to help people get up and reach their goals. If you help enough other people attain their goals, you will attain yours.

This principle is a classic form of a "win/win" situation. Both parties get what they want. The client gains a product that will meet a need. The sales representative receives a sale and possibly more money. There are no problems that hound a person in sales that a sale can't help. When the client happily purchases a product, the sales rep happily gains self-confidence. Do you want to renew your vigor in sales? If you do, begin helping more people.

When you help others you feel more than a sense of pride and security, you feel a sense of contribution. You are contributing to your community. You can find your greatness in God's community by helping someone else.

Discipline yourself to become a prayer warrior for others. You can drastically change someone's day through prayer. I try to pray with people as often as possible. One of the greatest opportunities that I have found is when I pray for my food. When I am in a restaurant and my food comes, I ask the server how I can pray for them when I thank God for my food. Generally, the person asks me to repeat myself. They have heard many comments, but few people take the time to show genuine concern for them. I have prayed for the sick, the dying, and for direction in life. After doing this for some time in the same restaurant, you will have the staff coming to ask you to pray for them.

Another key to praying for others is do not put off until later what you can do right now. Don't tell people, "I will remember you in my prayers." Stop and pray for them immediately. Have you ever told someone you would pray for the need and then forgot? I have. That is why I try to pray right away. Besides, I would rather pray with the person than in an impersonal way in private.

The more you pray with people, the more you will be like God. The Bible says when we do not know how to pray, as we ought, the Holy Spirit makes intercession for us with groanings too deep for words. Pray for others. Help other people get what they want. Prayer is not the least you can do for someone. It is absolutely the greatest way you can help.

No matter what degree of success you have achieved in sales, use your resources to help others. The Bible tells us true religion is taking care of widows and orphans. Are these the only people God wants us to help? The answer is obvious. Absolutely not! The principle God is teaching us is to take care of those who cannot care for themselves. In Jesus' day, widows and orphans were dependant on others to get the basics for human existence, water, food, and clothing. It was next to impossible for these people to care for themselves. They needed someone to care for them. If God's people will not take care of people like this, who will? God is counting on us to discover and meet these needs.

A principle I am learning is to give even when it hurts. Recently, God impressed on my heart to give some money to a family. The amount was very significant to me. It was all the cash I had in my pocket to take care of my family at a crucial time. Several things went through my mind. Am I really hearing from God? Maybe I should just give them half and I could keep half? I thought, "God, would it be okay if I did not obey you this time?" I even went to my wife hoping she would not agree with helping them. She immediately thought I should do it. I relented and gave the family the money. I knew I should do. Immediately, I felt at peace. Not a week later, someone gave me the exact amount I had given. Then a day later, I received five times the amount that I gave. God used others to bless my family. I would have missed a huge lesson if I had not been obedient. I want you to understand something clearly. Not every time I have given money to someone have I received a monetary blessing. Never give money to God to get something out of it. Give out of obedience, not greed. Let God decide what kind of blessing to give to you. You need to learn to give proportionally and sacrificially, according to what God has given to you.

Giving when it hurts is a blessing. I am so thankful that God gave his one and only Son to die for me. I am so thankful that at just the right time Jesus gave himself to die on the cross for the ungodly — including me. God gave a gift that hurt the most. He gave his life for you and me. Thank you God for helping me to achieve the one goal I could never attain on my own. Thank you for giving me eternal life in heaven.

Prayer Principle
Prayer is A Way of Helping Others

Dear Jesus,

Thank you for giving your best for me. Thank you for laying down your life willingly as a gift. Help me to give to others unselfishly. Allow me to become a person of generosity. Giving out of an abundant heart and a desire to serve others.

In Jesus' name,
Amen.

SEAL THE DEAL

Acknowledge Your Need of God in Your Prayers

Asking for the sale is both an art and a science. Statistics show that in both retail and direct marketing the percentage of sales significantly increase if the sales associates will ask for the sale. In fact, the research shows that sales reps only ask for the sale 50 percent of the time. The research of closing also proves you must learn specific techniques to achieve your goal, a sale. Closing the deal is hard for people new to sales. It seems pushy. However, if you do not ask for the sale, more times than not, there will not be a sale. You must learn how to help people want your product.

Closing is also an art. The selection of words should be direct but not aggressive. Aggressive techniques drive a wedge between you and the client. Direct techniques provide opportunities. Asking questions like, "May I wrap that item for you?" is a subtle but direct way of asking for the sale. A good statement for closing is, "All I need is your signature and I'll get the product ready for you." A retail close you can use is, "Would you like to take that home today?" For sales associates who do business in homes, you could say, "If you will get a check, I will finish the paperwork for you." All of these questions ask for the sale, but do not overwhelm the client.

When you ask for the sale, you need to do two things, smile and shut-up. Smile politely after you present your closing statement or question. Look expectantly and keep your mouth shut. An old saying is, "When you ask for the sale, the next person to speak loses." It may seem like an incredibly long time between your close and the client's yes or no. Nevertheless, if you speak, you will move the client away from the sale. You lose. If your product is as good as you say it is then the client is the loser as well. He or she does not have the opportunity to receive the benefits of your product. If you will sit and smile, the client will think about their response, and then let you know if they will buy.

Just as you have to ask for the sale, you must also ask God for your needs. Jesus taught people to pray, "Give us today, our daily bread." When we ask God for our needs, we are showing our dependence on him. Remember, God doesn't need our information. We need to acknowledge God as the provider of our needs.

God is interested in your needs. He says he knows you so well that he holds the number of hairs on your head in his memory. If God gives the flowers in the fields the most spectacular clothing to wear, how much more will he do for you. Since God promises to provide food and shelter for birds, do you not think he will care for you? For the things that we need, we are to trust in him. When you pray, seek first his kingdom and his righteousness. You do not have to worry about things that he has promised already to meet. Even though Jesus tells you to pray for your daily bread, he also tells you that the Father already knows your needs before you ask.

There is a big difference between worry and concern. Worry is when the problem so consumes you that you cannot go about your daily tasks. The word "concern" in late Latin meant "to perceive or comprehend." When you are concerned you learn to press on toward the ultimate spiritual goal in spite of the circumstances because your perception is that God is in control. Concern leads you to put the problem in God's hands and then trust him to do the right thing. Worry cripples you. Concern frees you. Concern moves you toward an answer for the problem. Worry hinders your ability to be God's workmanship created for good works.

God expects you to have faith in him when you pray. Faith is absolute belief that God is capable of doing the things he says he will do. When you have faith in the Lord, then you can pray, asking for whatever you need. Jesus says when you ask, believing, he will provide. He is a good Father, who provides the best for his children. He is not bound to provide our selfish desires. He certainly can bless in abundance.However, he will not always do it our way.

God is the great provider. If we know that he is at work to cause all things to work together for good, for those who are his children, then we will trust him fully. He has proven that the object that has the greatest value or the person with the most wealth is not impressive to him. What is important to God is the revealing to the world that he is real and that he loves each one of us. He wants to move our prayers to a place of belief. From the place of belief, God wants to reveal through us his love for the entire world. When we truly interact with God, others will want to interact with him the same way.

Sometimes asking God for personal needs is a tough thing to do. It is not as hard to ask for someone else's needs. For me, it is the idea that my father instilled in me as a young man. Take care of yourself and your family. Do not rely on anyone else. You are responsible for your family. You can use this idea negatively or positively. If you think that God is not interested in individuals, then you are on your own in this world. If you believe God is interested in everything about your life, you should acknowledge him at all times.

When asking for yourself, you must accept the uncomfortable to accomplish the incredible. If you want to be successful in sales, you have to ask for the client's business. If you want to grow in prayer, you boldly have to ask for your needs. God is concerned about you. He does want to show himself strong in the smallest details. If you begin to ask, with the heart of Christ, you will receive more than you can even imagine.

Prayer Principle
Acknowledge Your Need of God in Your Prayers

Dear Jesus,

I want to give you praise today because you are teaching me incredible things. Thank you for caring about every need in my life. I depend on you. Help me to seek your will, your kingdom, and your righteousness. Help me to be bold in my career. You have not given me a spirit of fear and timidity but one of power. Please, help me to have the confidence in myself and my product to ask my clients to purchase something I know that will help them.

In Jesus' name,
Amen.

TALK TO THE DECISION MAKER

God is the Ultimate Decision Maker in Prayer

Who in the world makes the decisions around here? If you are in sales, you had better figure out how to ask this question early in your presentation. If you go through your entire presentation and the decision maker is not present, you have wasted your time.

In order to get to the decision maker, you might have to go through a secretary. Here are some of my personal observations on this subject. Do not lie in order to talk to the decision maker. If you do, you will immediately lose credibility. Realize the decision maker gets dozens of calls a week like yours. Why does the decision maker want to talk to you? You must know the needs of the potential client and immediately give the client a reason to listen to you further. Do not act as if the potential client is a close friend or an acquaintance, if it is not true. The secretary and the client will refuse your future calls if this is your approach. I can promise you, you will not get my business if you mislead my secretary. We do communicate with one another about sales calls.

I was in the middle of a building program when I received one of the most ridiculous phone calls I have ever received. A secretary for a business that wanted the opportunity to bid on a segment of our building project called one day. She insisted that we must provide her the information for the contractor that won our business. Instead of being nice to my secretary, the woman made my secretary angry at the approach that was used. The woman who sought the information was rude and refused to listen to my secretary. She chastised my secretary and belittled our handling of our project. My secretary immediately informed me of the conversation and the company's name. Probably twenty minutes had not passed when the owner of the business called back. He insisted that I must give him the information and that I did not understand how the process of bidding worked. To his demise, I did understand the process and chose a closed bid process so I would not have to deal with the headaches of an open bid. The contractor continued to argue with me in spite of my best efforts to tell him I would not provide the information he wanted. Finally, out of frustration, he told me I was ruining my project. I had had enough. I informed him the project was mine to ruin in any way I liked. Furthermore, I informed him he would never work on a project for me now or in the future. His lack of listening to a decision maker cost him this and all future jobs. I am a client. I will be heard. It is my money to spend in any way that I choose. Do not talk down to me. Do not try to coerce me. Listen to what I have to say.

Once you get an opportunity to sit down with a potential client, discover whether one person or a team will make the final decision about buying. No one can make as good of a sales presentation as you can. If possible, do not let one of the decision makers relay your information to another person in the decision making process. You need to present your materials to the group, if the group makes the decisions to make purchases. What if one person in the decision making group dislikes the person who presents your material? You will not stand a chance of winning this group's business. If the decision is to be made by a husband and wife, don't sit down with one of them. You can't expect a spouse to convey your information effectively to the other spouse. Confirm that all decision makers will be at the table when you set your appointment.

When you pray, you know that the decision maker is listening to you. The Bible teaches that God is sovereign. The world we live in is under his control. He is actively involved with his creation. He wants to work on our behalf. There are times God simply interacts with our lives for our benefit. At other times, he wants us to acknowledge our needs to him.

When you trust God's judgment, you will accept his answers to your prayers. The will of God should always be what you seek. If you know that God will do what is right for his children, then when he answers your prayers differently than you expect, you accept his answers. Does

God love you? If you agree that he does, then he is going to do what is best for you.

Paul disclosed his trust in God's will when he told the people of Philippi that for him to live is Christ and to die is gain. He reminded others that the life that he lived was by faith in Christ. When he had the material things of life or when he had nothing, he was content. During times of suffering, he was willing to suffer as Jesus did.

No one exemplified trust in the Father's will more than Jesus. The most beautiful account of Jesus' trust in the Bible is the scene in the garden of Gethsemane. Jesus wrestled with the imminent sacrifice he would make for his followers. His struggle was so intense that sweat, like drops of blood, fell from his forehead. As he prayed for the removal of the cup that he was soon to drink, he prayed also for the Father's will to be done.

God's will is often different from our will. Our goal is to learn to surrender our will to his will. The words to a Garth Brooks song are, "some of God's greatest gifts are unanswered prayers." How many times have you prayed in a manner that was selfish, misdirected or uninformed? Learn to trust God's judgment. Learn to pray as Jesus did, "nevertheless may your will be done."

Prayer Principle
God is the Ultimate Decision Maker in Prayer

Dear Jesus,

I am overwhelmed by the access to the Father that you provide. Help me to understand your will and your ways. When I am weak, make me strong. When I lack understand, remind me to trust you. In my business, help me to help others so that through the blessings of my company and the financial rewards you give to me, I may point others to your peace, hope, mercy, and love.

In Jesus' name,
Amen.

NEGATIVE ANSWERS

Never Stop Trusting God. He is Faithful.

No does not mean never, just not now. When you view everyone as a client, you will change your outlook on sales. If someone has not bought your product or service, he or she has provided you with a future opportunity. Don't write off a potential client even if you have received a dozen negative answers. When someone says no, simply ask for permission to make contact later. You could say something like, "Thank you for taking a few minutes to consider my products today. With your permission, I will keep you in mind for new or improved products that might meet your needs or save you money."

Thomas Edison said, "Many of life's failures are men who did not realize how close they were to success when they gave up." In sales, you are only one more door away from a sale. So many people quit because of circumstances or criticism. Winning is the ability to get up one more time. When you quit, you can never produce a win. To produce a win you have to show up and give it your best every time, even if your best does not produce a win today.

You must not become content with the status quo. If you are going to succeed, you must do what others will not. "My great concern is not whether you have failed," said Abraham Lincoln, "but whether you are content with your failure." No matter how many times you hear no, even if many people are negative, you cannot become content with failure.

Every no leads you closer to a yes. Each company for whom I've consulted has crunched the numbers and knows how many clients you have to see, on average, to make a sale. So go see clients. Get belly-to-belly with ten people a week and you have the potential to make a lot of money in sales. Most sales reps never get this principle.

Another key is to receive a negative answer from a lot of qualified clients. Just anyone is not a potential client. You need to get in front of people who are highly qualified clients. When you master the goal of getting in front of ten highly qualified clients, you have the ability to increase your sales revenue exponentially.

If you are presenting your materials or products before highly qualified clients and you receive no for an answer, you should try to learn something from every no. If you begin to get many turn-downs for products or services, you may want to ask a client that you respect and who respects you for honest feedback. This is not something you want to do often or with just any client. Be extremely selective.

However, you might find out information that can lead to an affirmative answer and future sell. Appreciate all the no's you receive. You are one step closer to a yes.

When God tells us no, it is always for our best. However, just because God says no, does not mean he is saying never. Think of how many times Abraham and Sarah must have prayed for a child. Finally as a senior adult, 100 years old, God granted Abraham's request. God's timing is perfect timing and we must accept his answer. God might ask us to do something that is too big for us to comprehend at the time.

There was a time in my life when I had the opportunity to become the pastor of a church that was near my hometown. Everything about it seemed beneficial to me. It would provide a comfortable living and create an opportunity to reach many people. I could not understand why God would not allow me to say yes to a church that was just the kind of church I wanted to pastor. I still do not understand why God did not give me a peace about going there. However, I do know how God has blessed my obedience. God knows his dreams and desires for me. I do not. So I wait. And I trust.

Prayer is the life force to a faithful life. It is amazing that he considers our conversations worthy of his time and consideration. It is a constant reminder to me to respect, love, and cherish my time spent with him.

Jesus provided an illustration of persistent prayer, even in the face of an immediate answer of no or seemingly no response. Jesus said which of you, if you have unexpected company at midnight and need bread, would not go to a friend and ask for help. If the friend refuses because he is tired and doesn't want to get our of his bed, Jesus taught, that if you are persistent, the friend will get up and give you all you need (Luke 11:5-9).

In another example found in the book of Luke, Jesus describes a widow who begs for help against her enemies from a judge. The judge was not a God-fearer, nor did he fear people. However, the judge finally provided protection for the widow because she would not stop bringing her case before him. The judge gave in because the widow made him grow weary and finally resolved her case.

Both examples were provided to say to God's people, "Don't grow weary and lose heart." You are to pray until you have a clear answer from God. Until you have the answer, continue to beg and plead your case before the righteous judge. It is not that God forgets. On the contrary, sometimes it is God who does not want you to forget who provides the answers to prayer.

Just as you learn from a no in sales, you can learn from a no by God. Seek the answer to the questions of why, how, when, or what. Why are you saying no at this time, God? How are you trying to prepare me for something else or to receive a positive answer later? When is it appropriate for me to ask again? When do you want me to find out why your answer is no? What are you teaching me? What do you want me to learn? What do you want me to do in the meantime?

Trust God's answer and learn to lean on him. In all your ways acknowledge him and he will direct your paths. God knows the plans he has for you. He always seeks to prosper his children and not to harm them. That doesn't mean you will always be rich and unencumbered by the cares of the world. However, it does mean that God will seek your best in the midst of his plan. If in the course of the evil that is in this world, you find yourself struggling, or if God wants to use your tragedy as a triumphant testimony, place yourself in the hands of a trustworthy God.

God is trustworthy in all aspects of your life. Give him your sales career to be used for his glory. Give him your family. Give him your recreation. Give him your worship. Give him your praise. Give him your all. Let him use even a no to bring his glory and peace to the nations through you.

Prayer Principle
Never Stop Trusting God. He is Faithful.

Dear Jesus,

Thank you that you are an all-powerful, all-loving God. Thank you that your answers to my prayers are always the perfect answer for those for whom I pray and for me. God, I give you my career in sales. I will work hard to honor you. I will work smart to honor you. I will grow to honor you. Thank you that even when I hear the word no, I am one step closer to helping someone with the gifts and abilities you've given to me.

In Jesus' name,
Amen.

Afterword

Other Resources @ KeithManuel.com

I'm thrilled you've chosen a career in sales. I'm even more ecstatic that you chose to read *The Praying Sales Rep*. My prayer is that these 18 power principles will explode your career and more importantly your prayer life. God really wants to use your life to affect His world.

I want to personally invite you to visit KeithManuel. com. On it, you can explore resources for evangelism and disciplemaking that I've used personally. They are linked to the company or author who created them. Some have a minimal cost. Others are free. I will update and try my best to keep all the links and resources current.

I would love to hear an update about the progress of your prayer life and your sales career. Send me a prayer request or drop a note about life. I will be honored to pray with you.

There is a contact section on KeithManuel.com or you can email direct at Keith@KeithManuel.com.

Finally, check the website for additional books that are coming soon. I am working on a book of Bible verses and quotations to encourage our Law Enforcement Officers, First Responders, and anyone on the front line of serving our communities and nation.

Also, I am working on a book for strengthening marriages. It is a proven concept I have used with hundreds of couples.

God bless you as you lead your sales team (even if you are a team of one) and as you attempt to live your life for our Lord, Jesus Christ. I pray you will press forward under the power and work of the Holy Spirit.

Keith Manuel

About the Author

Keith Manuel is an emerging author for church ministries, families, and children. His numerous articles appear in church related publications.

His book, *The Desperate Church*, has helped congregations big and small reflect how the Holy Spirit is leading them to shine the light of Jesus in their communities. It is a tool that has seen churches develop a renewed vision and regain their strength.

He edited *One on One: Evangelism Made Simple* and created the website WhatIValueMost.com (Read his story there). He edited three devotional guides for Louisiana Baptists. Keith has served as a pastor, professor, photographer, and denominational consultant (Sorry. No "P" for that one!).

Hundreds of churches use Keith to speak and consult in areas of evangelism, revitalization, and encouragement. Visit his website at KeithManuel.com for booking information.

Keith is a graduate of William Carey University (B.A.) and New Orleans Baptist Theological Seminary (M.Div.; Th.M.; & Ph.D.). He is married to Wendy. They have three children Keith, Jr., Jeremy, and Hannah.

Available Now

THE DESPERATE CHURCH

SO MANY QUESTIONS. SO LITTLE TIME.
MY CHURCH IS HURTING.

KEITH MANUEL

ASKING GOD FOR A FRESH START
THROUGH PRAYER AND PLANNING

A powerful tool for any congregation or church
member who needs a renewed vision
for their ministry.

NOTES

NOTES

NOTES

NOTES

NOTES

NOTES

www.ingramcontent.com/pod-product-compliance
Lightning Source LLC
Chambersburg PA
CBHW020041040426
42331CB00030B/123